My First Book About OUTER SPACE

Donald M. Silver

and

Patricia J. Wynne

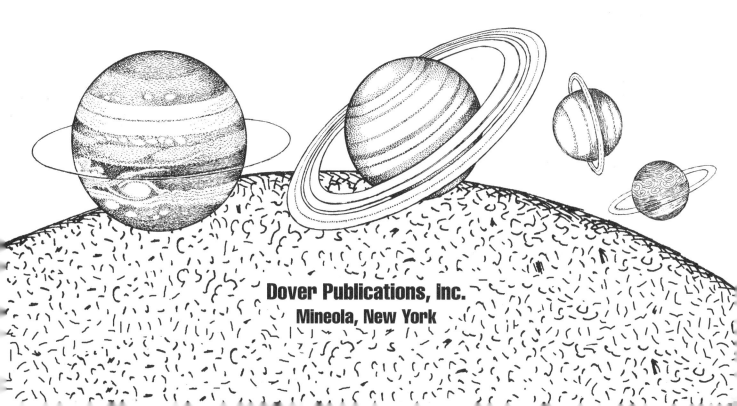

Dover Publications, Inc.

Mineola, New York

*We would like to dedicate this book to
Jewell Wood Wynne, whose love of the stars is eternal.*
Patricia Wynne and Donald Silver

In this fun and fact-filled coloring book, you will learn all about our Solar System and the planets in it. Discover how the Sun works, the history of the moon, and why Earth is able to support life. Plus, you will find out amazing information on comets, meteors, constellations, and black holes, among many other outer space phenomena. So get your crayons, markers, and colored pencils ready as you take a trip to the stars!

Bibliographical Note
My First Book About Outer Space is a new work, first published by
Dover Publications, Inc., in 2015.

International Standard Book Number
ISBN-13: 978-0-486-78329-1
ISBN-10: 0-486-78329-4

Manufactured in the United States by Courier Corporation
78329401   2015
www.doverpublications.com

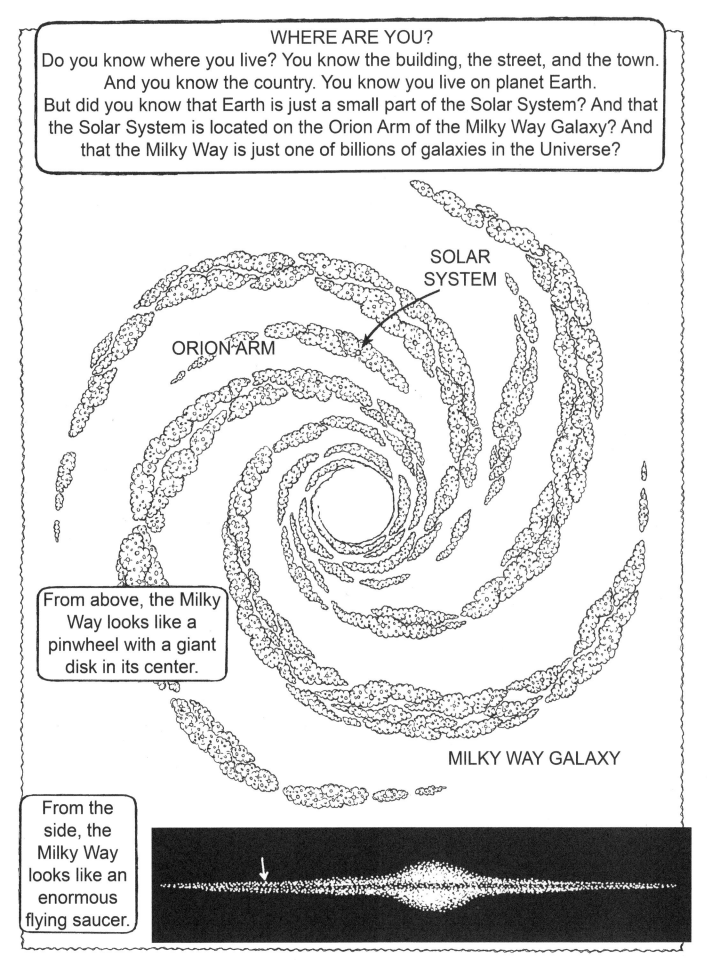

WHERE ARE YOU?
Do you know where you live? You know the building, the street, and the town. And you know the country. You know you live on planet Earth.
But did you know that Earth is just a small part of the Solar System? And that the Solar System is located on the Orion Arm of the Milky Way Galaxy? And that the Milky Way is just one of billions of galaxies in the Universe?

SOLAR SYSTEM

ORION ARM

From above, the Milky Way looks like a pinwheel with a giant disk in its center.

MILKY WAY GALAXY

From the side, the Milky Way looks like an enormous flying saucer.

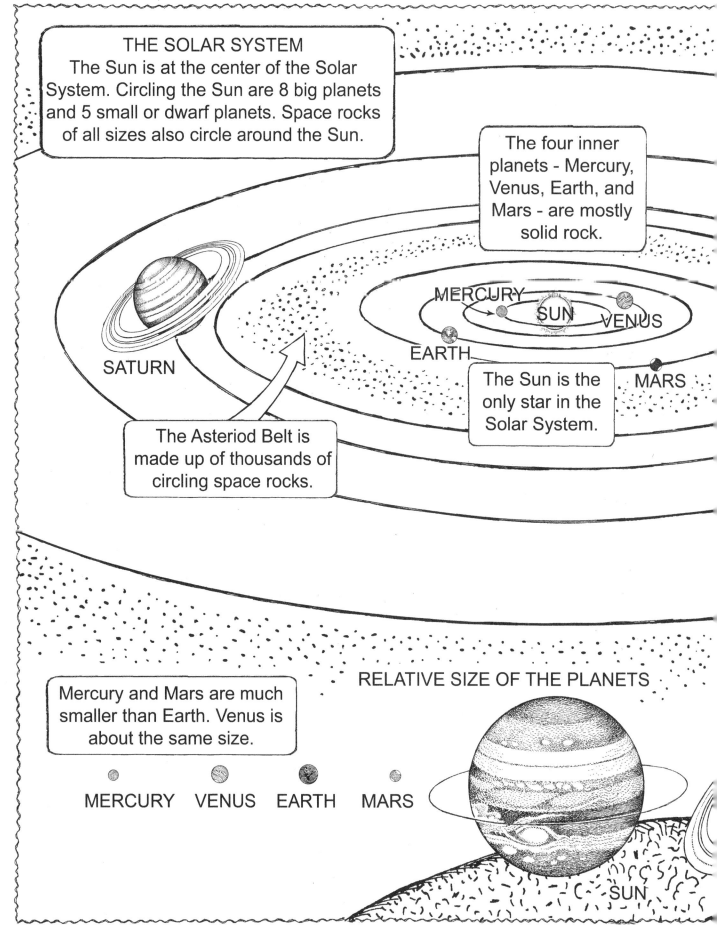

THE SOLAR SYSTEM
The Sun is at the center of the Solar System. Circling the Sun are 8 big planets and 5 small or dwarf planets. Space rocks of all sizes also circle around the Sun.

The four inner planets - Mercury, Venus, Earth, and Mars - are mostly solid rock.

The Asteriod Belt is made up of thousands of circling space rocks.

SATURN

MERCURY

SUN

VENUS

EARTH

MARS

The Sun is the only star in the Solar System.

Mercury and Mars are much smaller than Earth. Venus is about the same size.

RELATIVE SIZE OF THE PLANETS

MERCURY   VENUS   EARTH   MARS

SUN

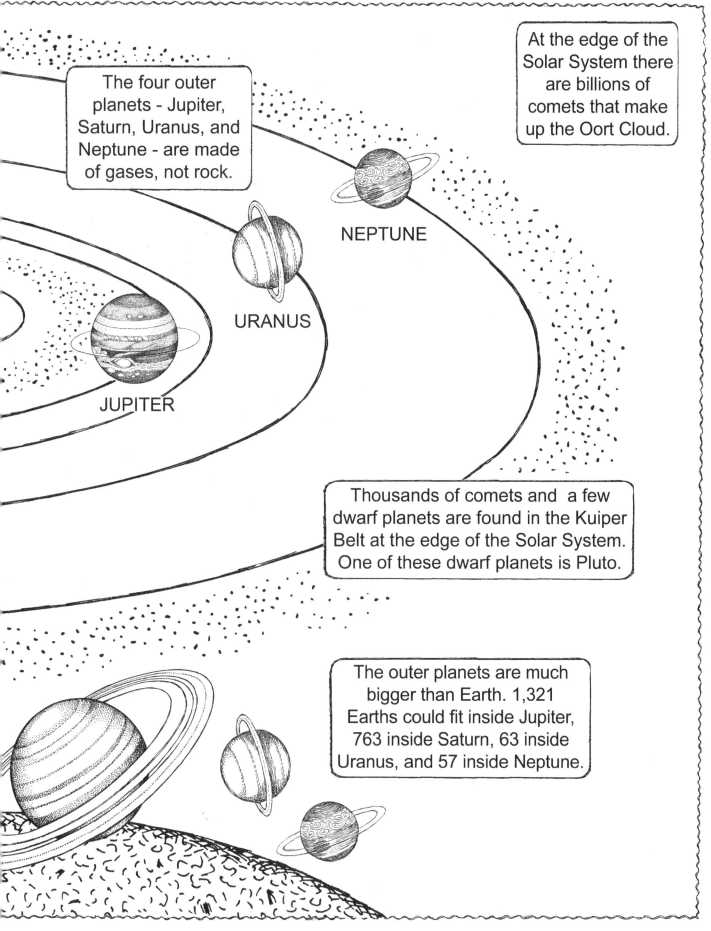

The four outer planets - Jupiter, Saturn, Uranus, and Neptune - are made of gases, not rock.

At the edge of the Solar System there are billions of comets that make up the Oort Cloud.

NEPTUNE

URANUS

JUPITER

Thousands of comets and a few dwarf planets are found in the Kuiper Belt at the edge of the Solar System. One of these dwarf planets is Pluto.

The outer planets are much bigger than Earth. 1,321 Earths could fit inside Jupiter, 763 inside Saturn, 63 inside Uranus, and 57 inside Neptune.

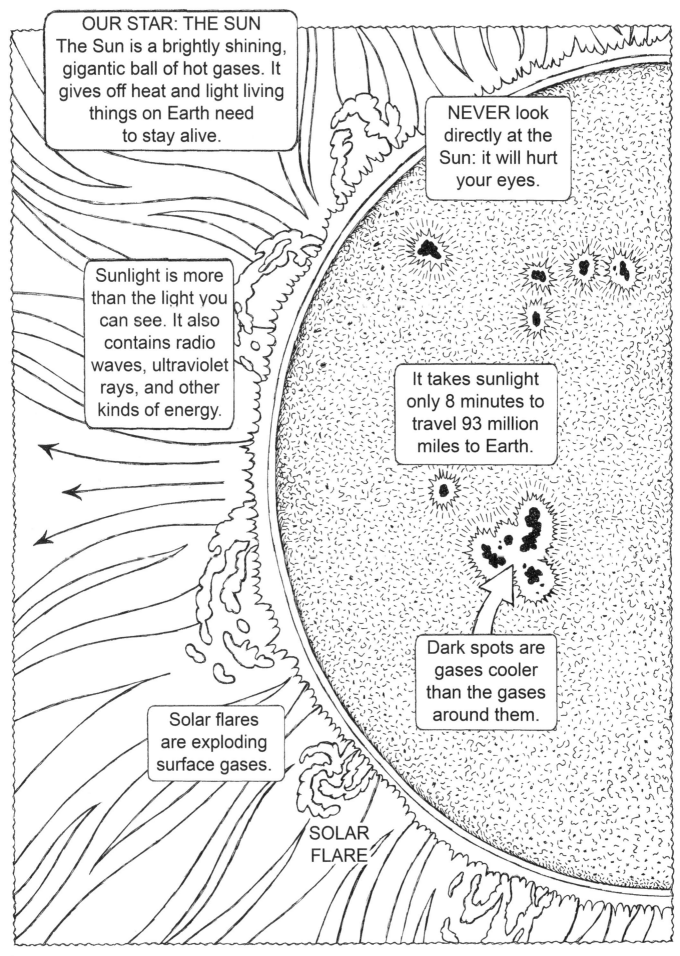

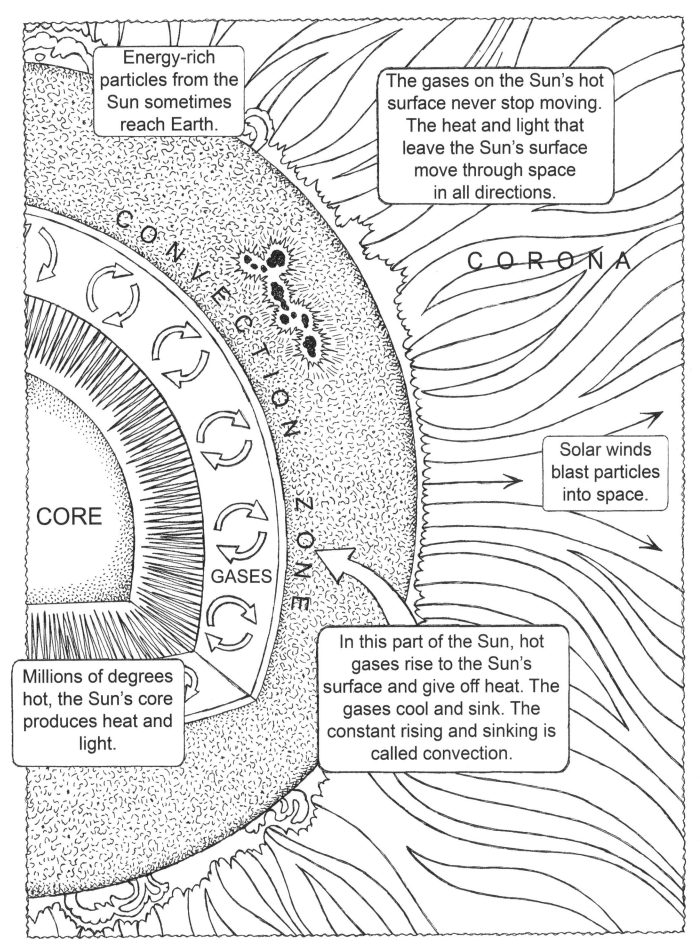

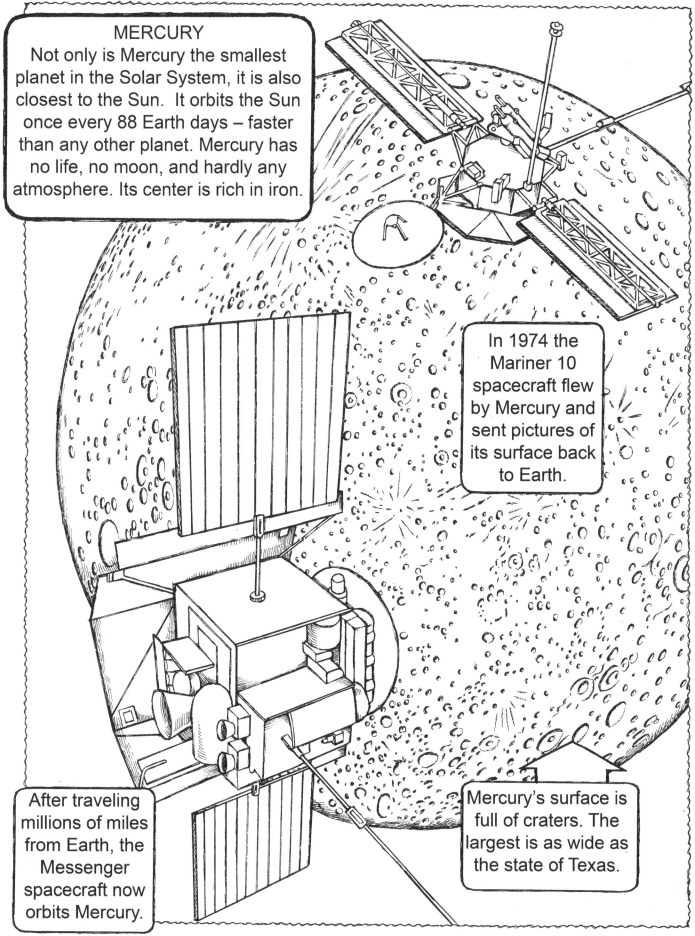

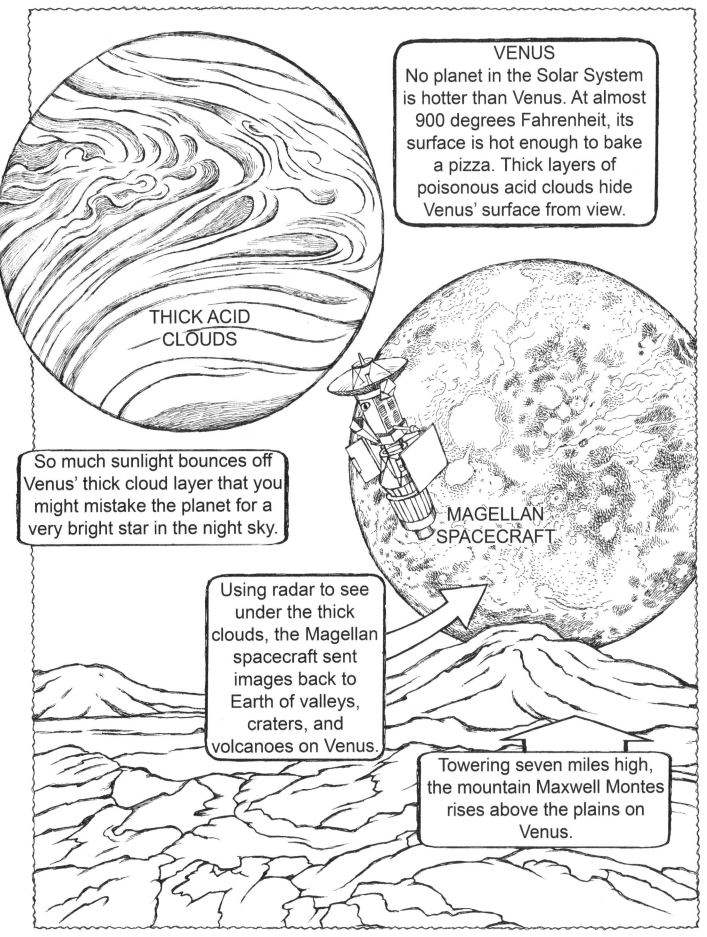

VENUS
No planet in the Solar System is hotter than Venus. At almost 900 degrees Fahrenheit, its surface is hot enough to bake a pizza. Thick layers of poisonous acid clouds hide Venus' surface from view.

THICK ACID CLOUDS

So much sunlight bounces off Venus' thick cloud layer that you might mistake the planet for a very bright star in the night sky.

MAGELLAN SPACECRAFT

Using radar to see under the thick clouds, the Magellan spacecraft sent images back to Earth of valleys, craters, and volcanoes on Venus.

Towering seven miles high, the mountain Maxwell Montes rises above the plains on Venus.

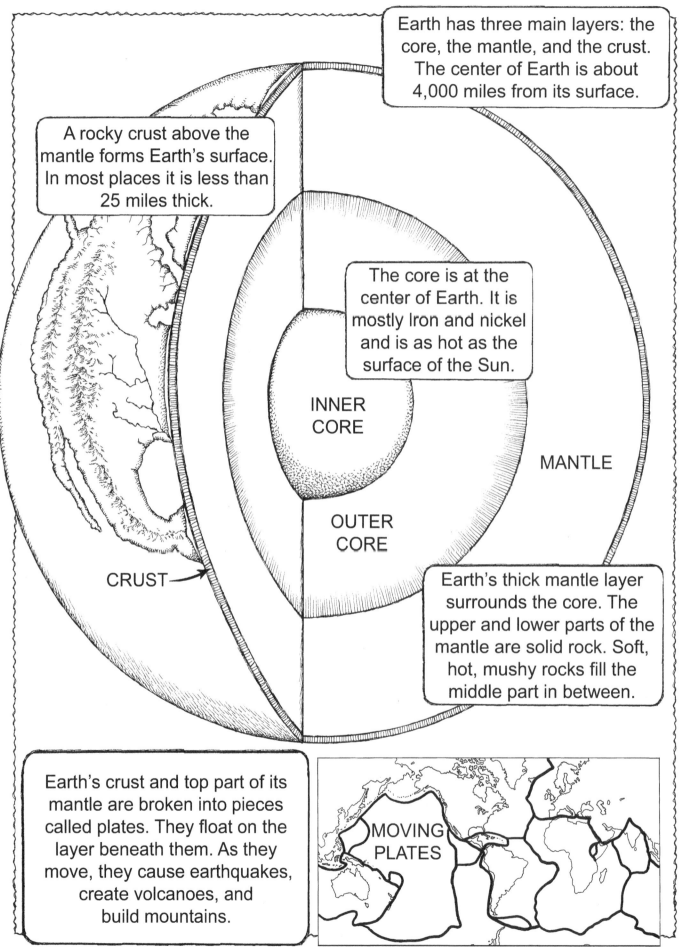

Earth has three main layers: the core, the mantle, and the crust. The center of Earth is about 4,000 miles from its surface.

A rocky crust above the mantle forms Earth's surface. In most places it is less than 25 miles thick.

The core is at the center of Earth. It is mostly Iron and nickel and is as hot as the surface of the Sun.

INNER CORE

MANTLE

OUTER CORE

CRUST

Earth's thick mantle layer surrounds the core. The upper and lower parts of the mantle are solid rock. Soft, hot, mushy rocks fill the middle part in between.

Earth's crust and top part of its mantle are broken into pieces called plates. They float on the layer beneath them. As they move, they cause earthquakes, create volcanoes, and build mountains.

MOVING PLATES

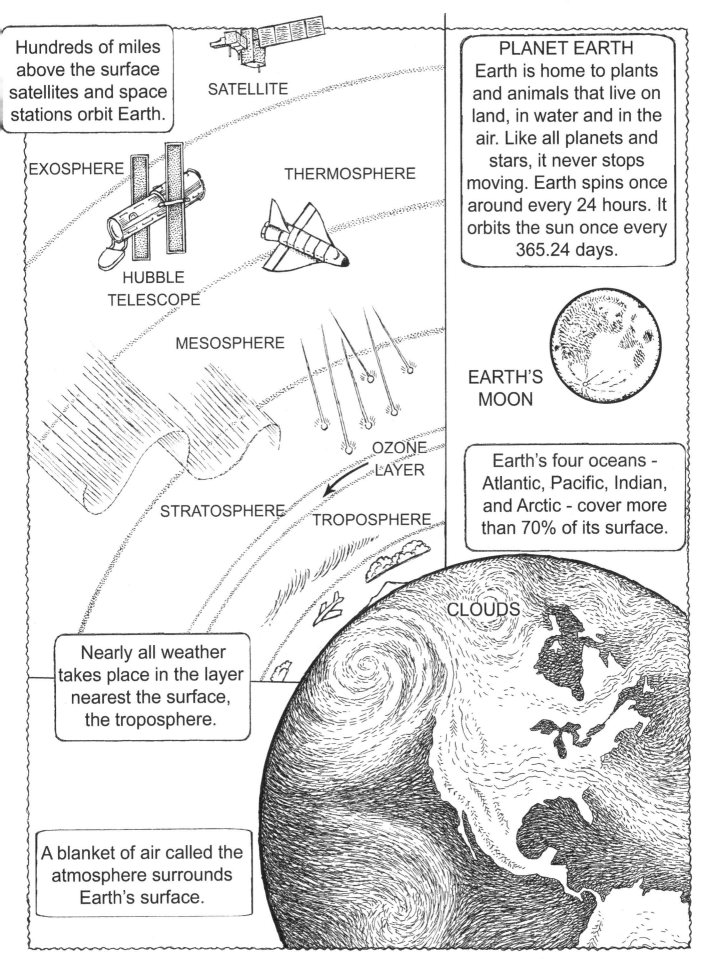

Hundreds of miles above the surface satellites and space stations orbit Earth.

SATELLITE

EXOSPHERE

THERMOSPHERE

HUBBLE
TELESCOPE

MESOSPHERE

OZONE
LAYER

STRATOSPHERE

TROPOSPHERE

Nearly all weather takes place in the layer nearest the surface, the troposphere.

A blanket of air called the atmosphere surrounds Earth's surface.

PLANET EARTH
Earth is home to plants and animals that live on land, in water and in the air. Like all planets and stars, it never stops moving. Earth spins once around every 24 hours. It orbits the sun once every 365.24 days.

EARTH'S
MOON

Earth's four oceans - Atlantic, Pacific, Indian, and Arctic - cover more than 70% of its surface.

CLOUDS

9

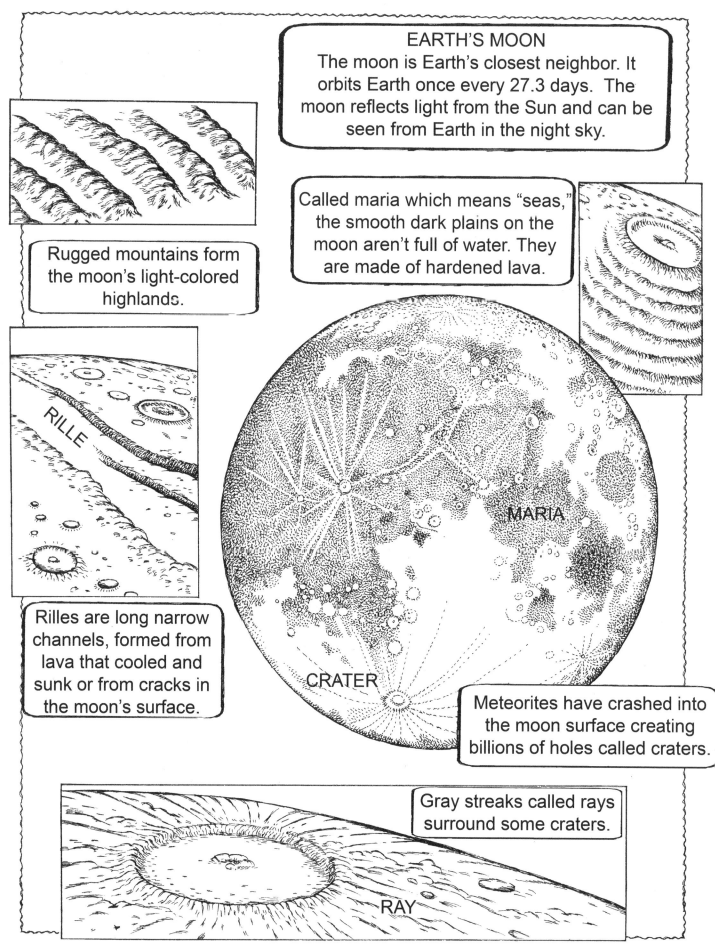

EARTH'S MOON
The moon is Earth's closest neighbor. It orbits Earth once every 27.3 days. The moon reflects light from the Sun and can be seen from Earth in the night sky.

Rugged mountains form the moon's light-colored highlands.

Called maria which means "seas," the smooth dark plains on the moon aren't full of water. They are made of hardened lava.

RILLE

Rilles are long narrow channels, formed from lava that cooled and sunk or from cracks in the moon's surface.

MARIA

CRATER

Meteorites have crashed into the moon surface creating billions of holes called craters.

Gray streaks called rays surround some craters.

RAY

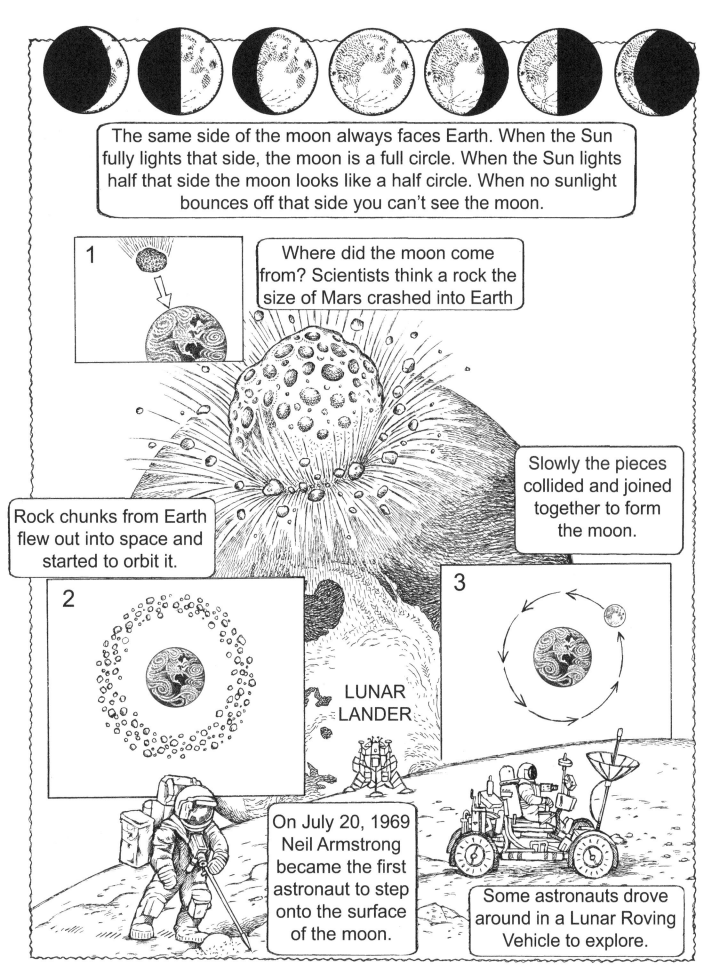

The same side of the moon always faces Earth. When the Sun fully lights that side, the moon is a full circle. When the Sun lights half that side the moon looks like a half circle. When no sunlight bounces off that side you can't see the moon.

1

Where did the moon come from? Scientists think a rock the size of Mars crashed into Earth

Slowly the pieces collided and joined together to form the moon.

Rock chunks from Earth flew out into space and started to orbit it.

2

3

LUNAR LANDER

On July 20, 1969 Neil Armstrong became the first astronaut to step onto the surface of the moon.

Some astronauts drove around in a Lunar Roving Vehicle to explore.

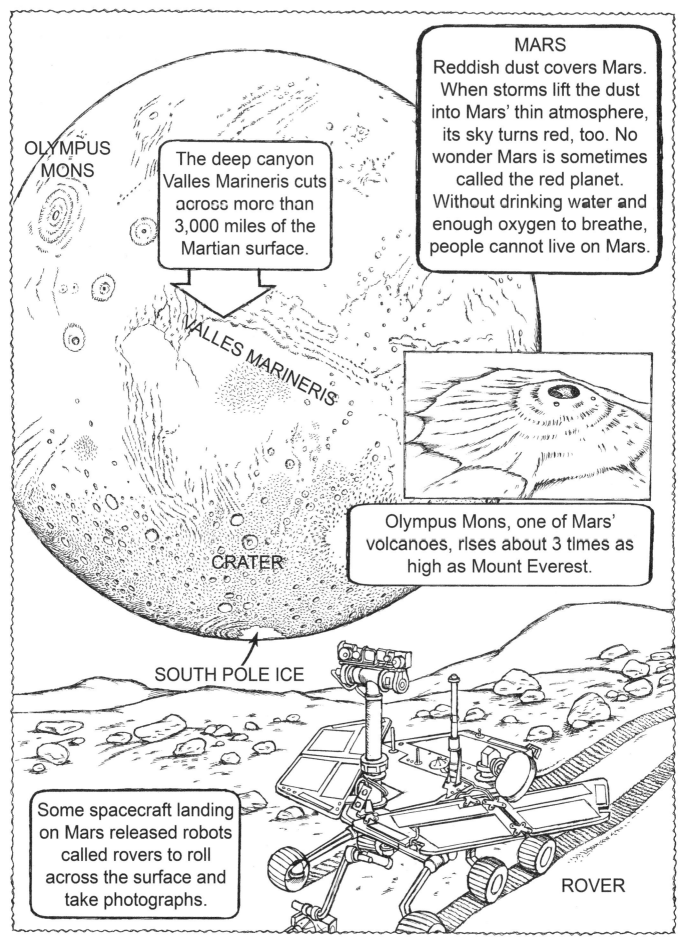

OLYMPUS MONS

The deep canyon Valles Marineris cuts across more than 3,000 miles of the Martian surface.

MARS
Reddish dust covers Mars. When storms lift the dust into Mars' thin atmosphere, its sky turns red, too. No wonder Mars is sometimes called the red planet. Without drinking water and enough oxygen to breathe, people cannot live on Mars.

VALLES MARINERIS

CRATER

Olympus Mons, one of Mars' volcanoes, rises about 3 times as high as Mount Everest.

SOUTH POLE ICE

Some spacecraft landing on Mars released robots called rovers to roll across the surface and take photographs.

ROVER

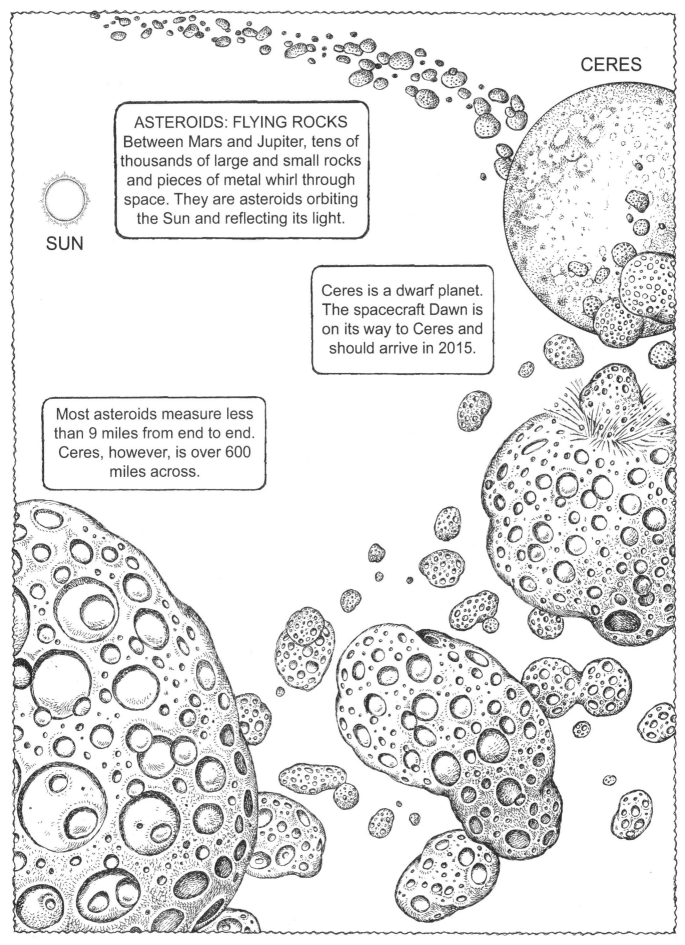

CERES

ASTEROIDS: FLYING ROCKS
Between Mars and Jupiter, tens of thousands of large and small rocks and pieces of metal whirl through space. They are asteroids orbiting the Sun and reflecting its light.

SUN

Ceres is a dwarf planet. The spacecraft Dawn is on its way to Ceres and should arrive in 2015.

Most asteroids measure less than 9 miles from end to end. Ceres, however, is over 600 miles across.

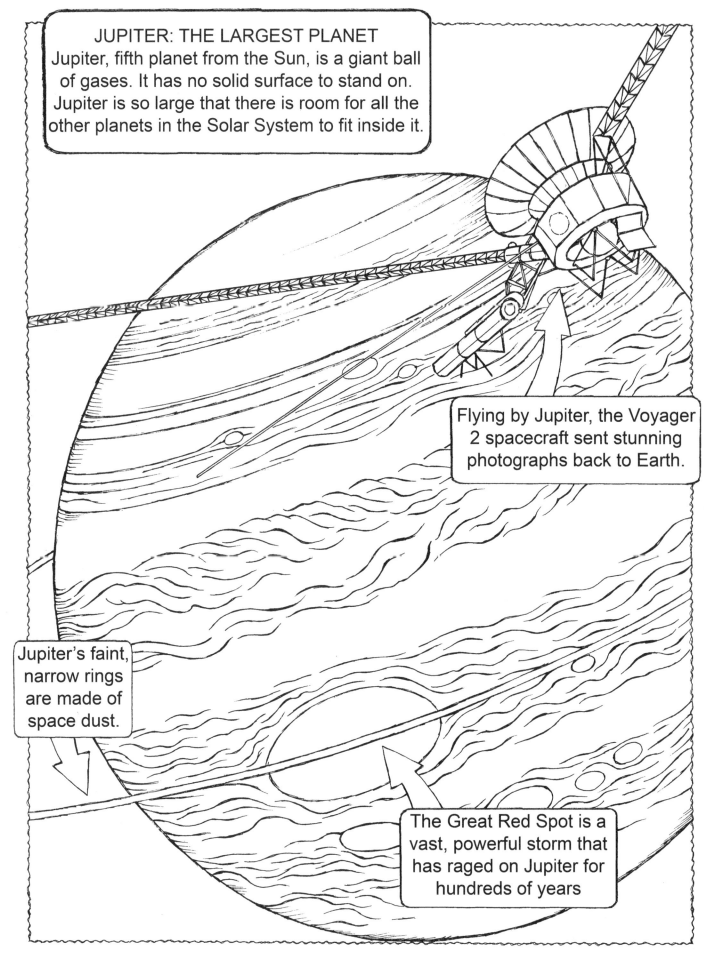

JUPITER: THE LARGEST PLANET
Jupiter, fifth planet from the Sun, is a giant ball of gases. It has no solid surface to stand on. Jupiter is so large that there is room for all the other planets in the Solar System to fit inside it.

Flying by Jupiter, the Voyager 2 spacecraft sent stunning photographs back to Earth.

Jupiter's faint, narrow rings are made of space dust.

The Great Red Spot is a vast, powerful storm that has raged on Jupiter for hundreds of years

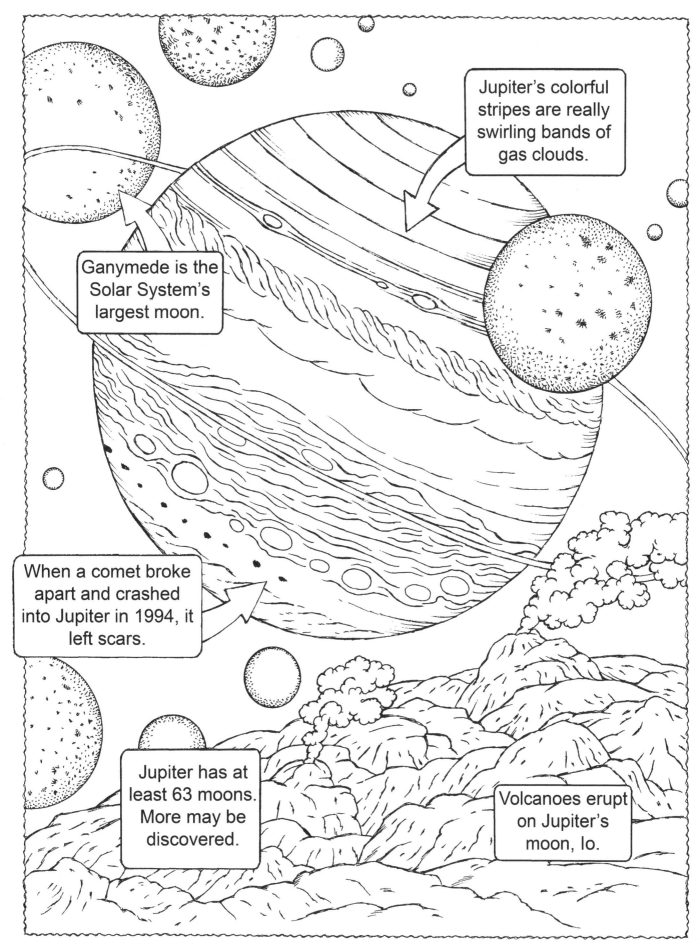

SATURN AND ITS RINGS
With its dazzling rings, Saturn is the second
largest planet in the Solar System. Like Jupiter, it
is a giant ball of gases. Saturn would float in a
tub of water if there was one big enough.

Titan, the largest of
Saturn's 53
moons, is bigger
than the planet
Mercury.

TITAN

CASSINI

HUYGENS
LANDER

The Cassini spacecraft has been
orbiting Saturn since 2004. When
the Huygens Lander was launched
from Cassini, it floated to the
surface of Titan using a parachute.

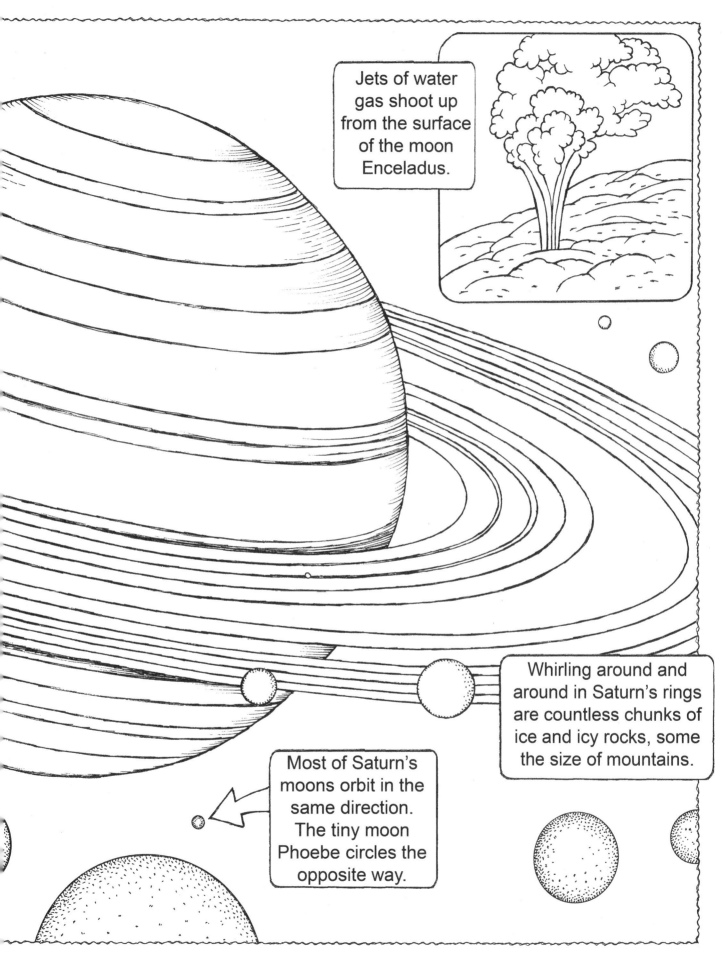

17

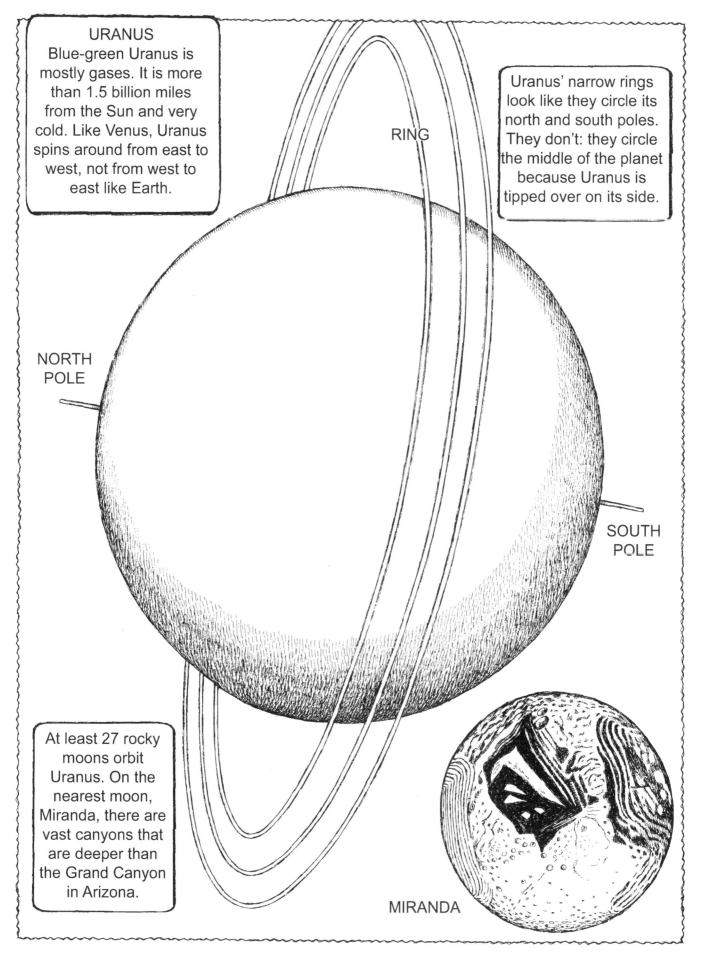

URANUS
Blue-green Uranus is mostly gases. It is more than 1.5 billion miles from the Sun and very cold. Like Venus, Uranus spins around from east to west, not from west to east like Earth.

Uranus' narrow rings look like they circle its north and south poles. They don't: they circle the middle of the planet because Uranus is tipped over on its side.

RING

NORTH POLE

SOUTH POLE

At least 27 rocky moons orbit Uranus. On the nearest moon, Miranda, there are vast canyons that are deeper than the Grand Canyon in Arizona.

MIRANDA

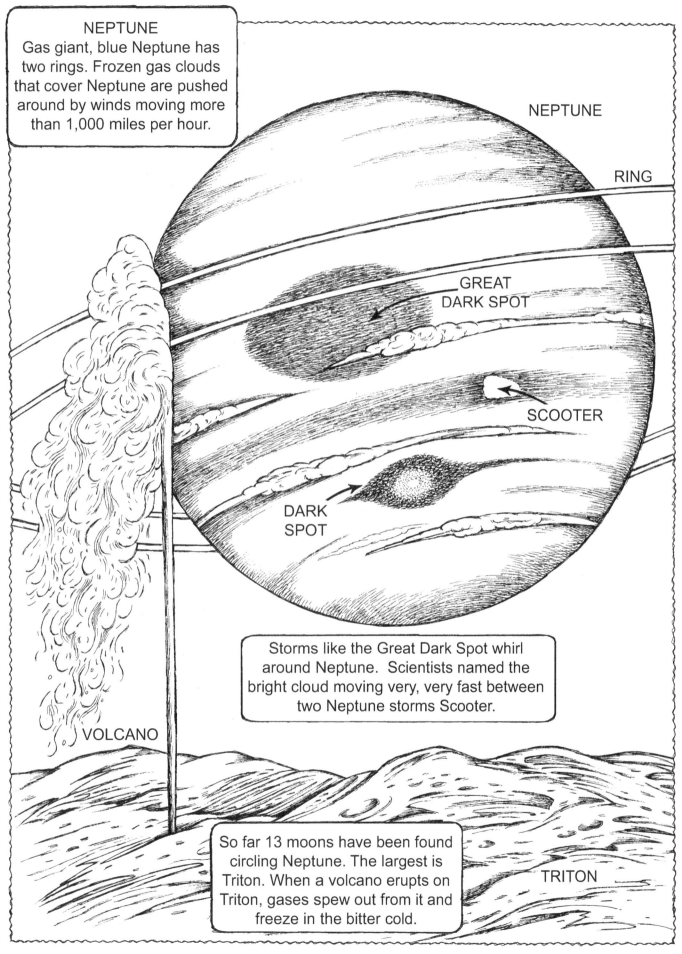

NEPTUNE
Gas giant, blue Neptune has two rings. Frozen gas clouds that cover Neptune are pushed around by winds moving more than 1,000 miles per hour.

NEPTUNE

RING

GREAT DARK SPOT

SCOOTER

DARK SPOT

Storms like the Great Dark Spot whirl around Neptune. Scientists named the bright cloud moving very, very fast between two Neptune storms Scooter.

VOLCANO

So far 13 moons have been found circling Neptune. The largest is Triton. When a volcano erupts on Triton, gases spew out from it and freeze in the bitter cold.

TRITON

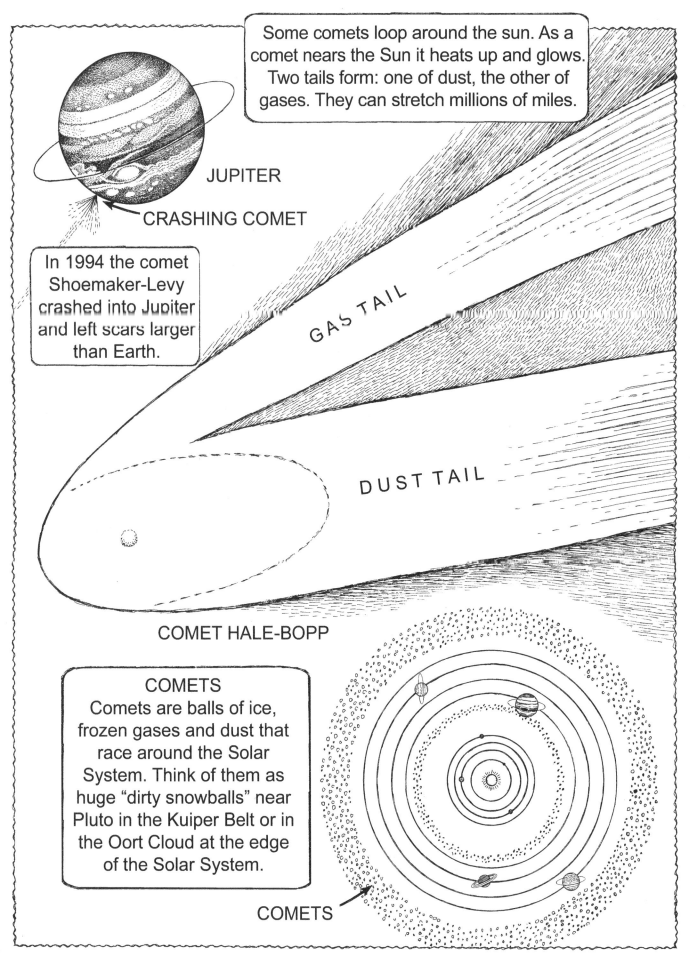

Some comets loop around the sun. As a comet nears the Sun it heats up and glows. Two tails form: one of dust, the other of gases. They can stretch millions of miles.

JUPITER

CRASHING COMET

In 1994 the comet Shoemaker-Levy crashed into Jupiter and left scars larger than Earth.

GAS TAIL

DUST TAIL

COMET HALE-BOPP

COMETS
Comets are balls of ice, frozen gases and dust that race around the Solar System. Think of them as huge "dirty snowballs" near Pluto in the Kuiper Belt or in the Oort Cloud at the edge of the Solar System.

COMETS

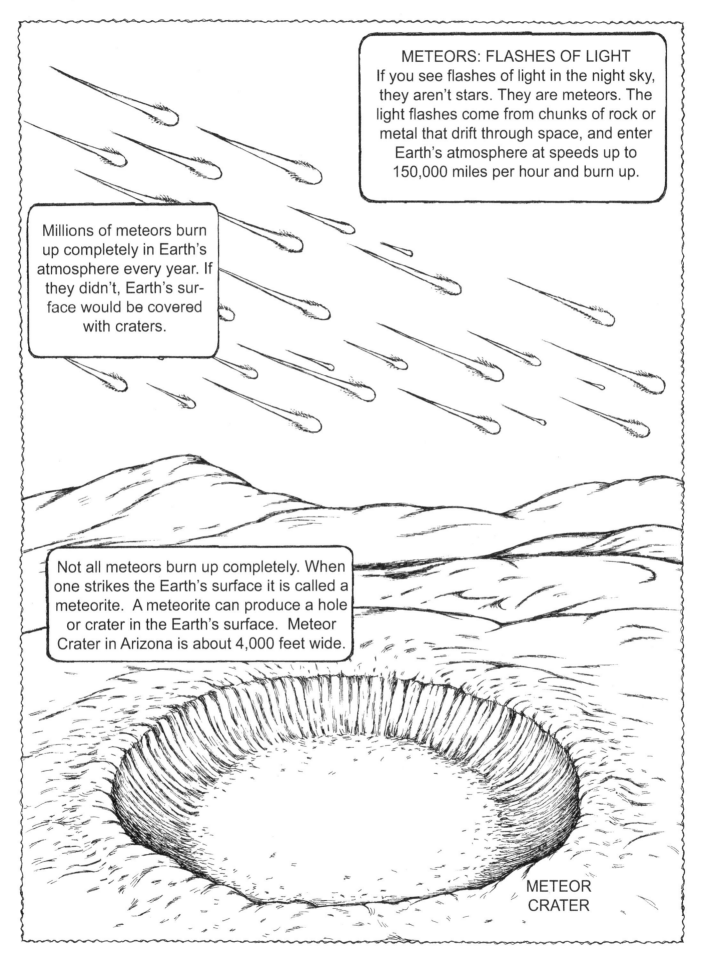

METEORS: FLASHES OF LIGHT
If you see flashes of light in the night sky, they aren't stars. They are meteors. The light flashes come from chunks of rock or metal that drift through space, and enter Earth's atmosphere at speeds up to 150,000 miles per hour and burn up.

Millions of meteors burn up completely in Earth's atmosphere every year. If they didn't, Earth's surface would be covered with craters.

Not all meteors burn up completely. When one strikes the Earth's surface it is called a meteorite. A meteorite can produce a hole or crater in the Earth's surface. Meteor Crater in Arizona is about 4,000 feet wide.

METEOR CRATER

WHAT HAPPENED TO THE DINOSAURS?
About 65 million years ago Earth's dinosaurs became extinct – they died off forever. So did about 75% of all the kinds of plants and other animals alive then. About 65 million years ago a comet or an asteroid crashed into Earth.

Did the crash blast tons of rocks into the air? Did the falling rocks start raging fires? Did dust and smoke fill the air for months, block sunlight, and bring on a long winter? Most scientists think so.

Scientists think land plants died because they could not make food. Plant-eaters starved. The animals that fed on the plant-eaters did too. Most animals that lived underground and stored food survived.

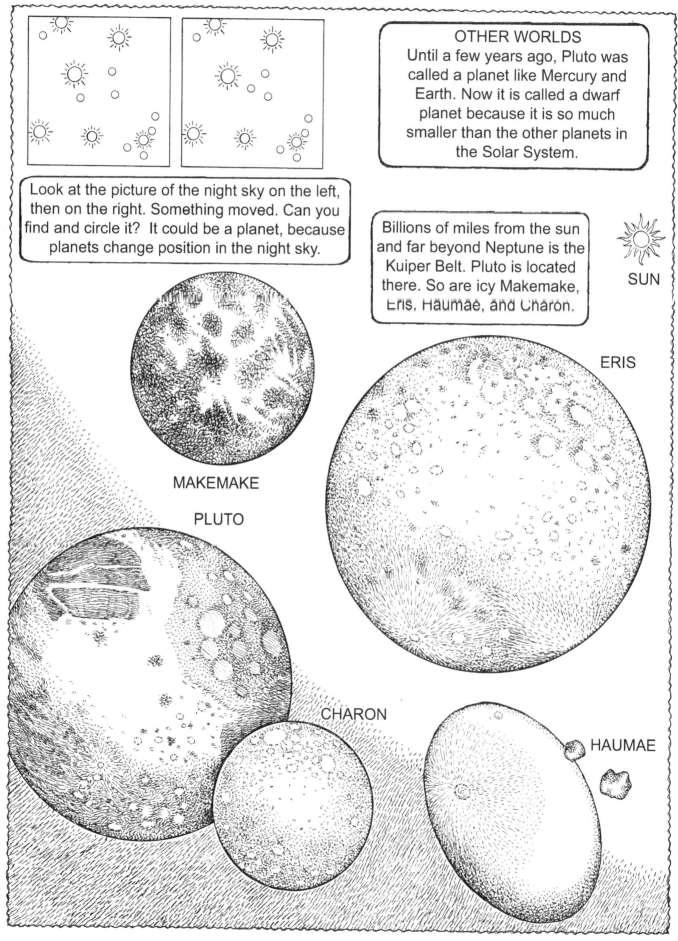

OTHER WORLDS
Until a few years ago, Pluto was called a planet like Mercury and Earth. Now it is called a dwarf planet because it is so much smaller than the other planets in the Solar System.

Look at the picture of the night sky on the left, then on the right. Something moved. Can you find and circle it? It could be a planet, because planets change position in the night sky.

Billions of miles from the sun and far beyond Neptune is the Kuiper Belt. Pluto is located there. So are icy Makemake, Eris, Haumae, and Charon.

SUN

MAKEMAKE

ERIS

PLUTO

CHARON

HAUMAE

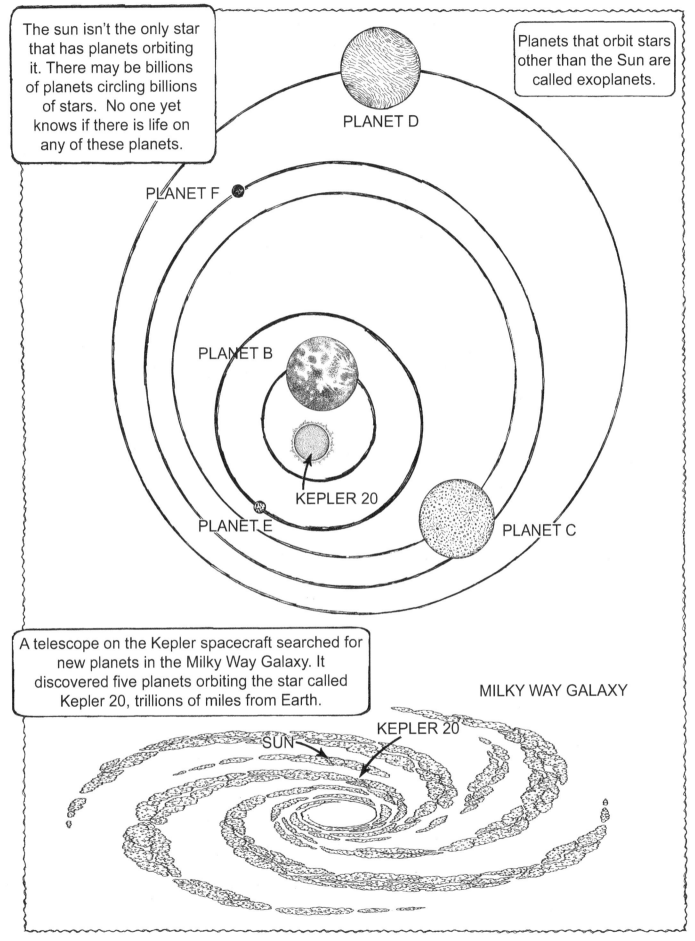

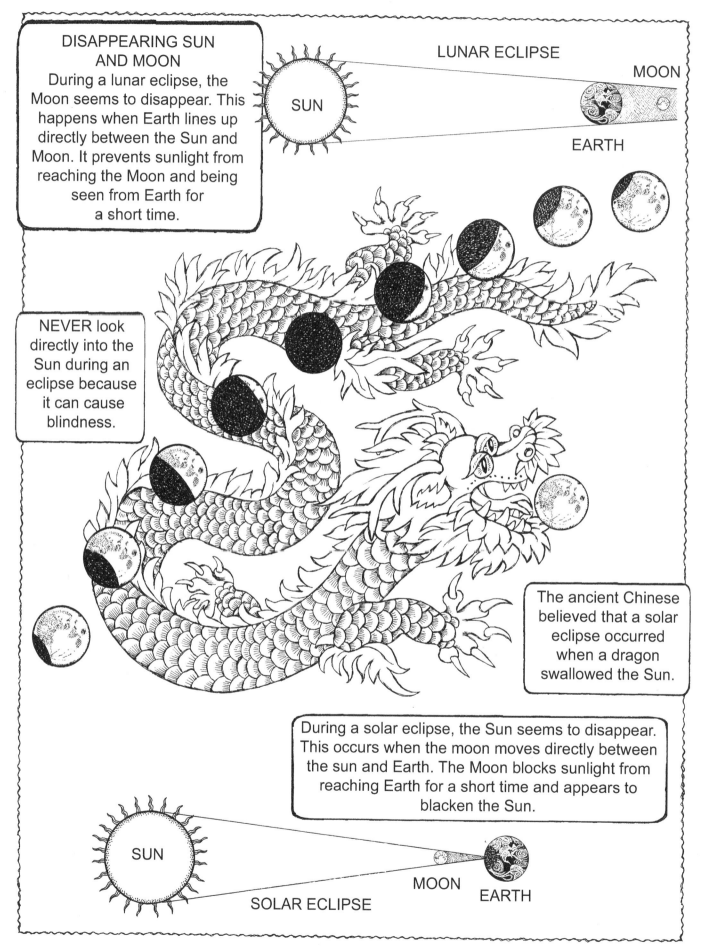

DISAPPEARING SUN AND MOON
During a lunar eclipse, the Moon seems to disappear. This happens when Earth lines up directly between the Sun and Moon. It prevents sunlight from reaching the Moon and being seen from Earth for a short time.

LUNAR ECLIPSE

MOON

SUN

EARTH

NEVER look directly into the Sun during an eclipse because it can cause blindness.

The ancient Chinese believed that a solar eclipse occurred when a dragon swallowed the Sun.

During a solar eclipse, the Sun seems to disappear. This occurs when the moon moves directly between the sun and Earth. The Moon blocks sunlight from reaching Earth for a short time and appears to blacken the Sun.

SUN

MOON   EARTH

SOLAR ECLIPSE

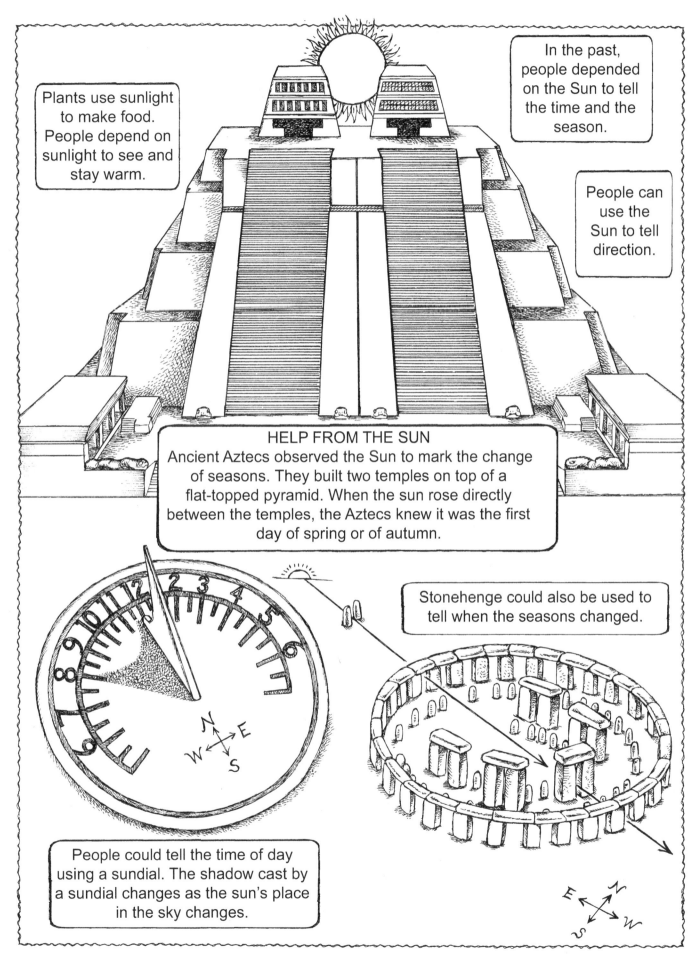

Plants use sunlight to make food. People depend on sunlight to see and stay warm.

In the past, people depended on the Sun to tell the time and the season.

People can use the Sun to tell direction.

HELP FROM THE SUN
Ancient Aztecs observed the Sun to mark the change of seasons. They built two temples on top of a flat-topped pyramid. When the sun rose directly between the temples, the Aztecs knew it was the first day of spring or of autumn.

Stonehenge could also be used to tell when the seasons changed.

People could tell the time of day using a sundial. The shadow cast by a sundial changes as the sun's place in the sky changes.

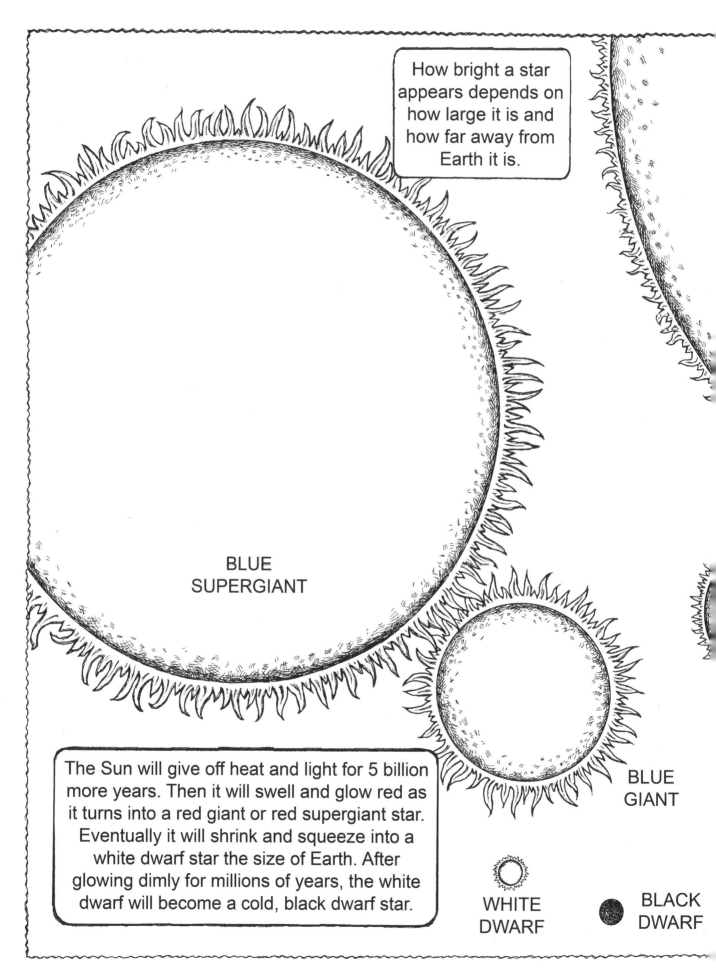

How bright a star appears depends on how large it is and how far away from Earth it is.

BLUE
SUPERGIANT

BLUE
GIANT

The Sun will give off heat and light for 5 billion more years. Then it will swell and glow red as it turns into a red giant or red supergiant star. Eventually it will shrink and squeeze into a white dwarf star the size of Earth. After glowing dimly for millions of years, the white dwarf will become a cold, black dwarf star.

WHITE
DWARF

BLACK
DWARF

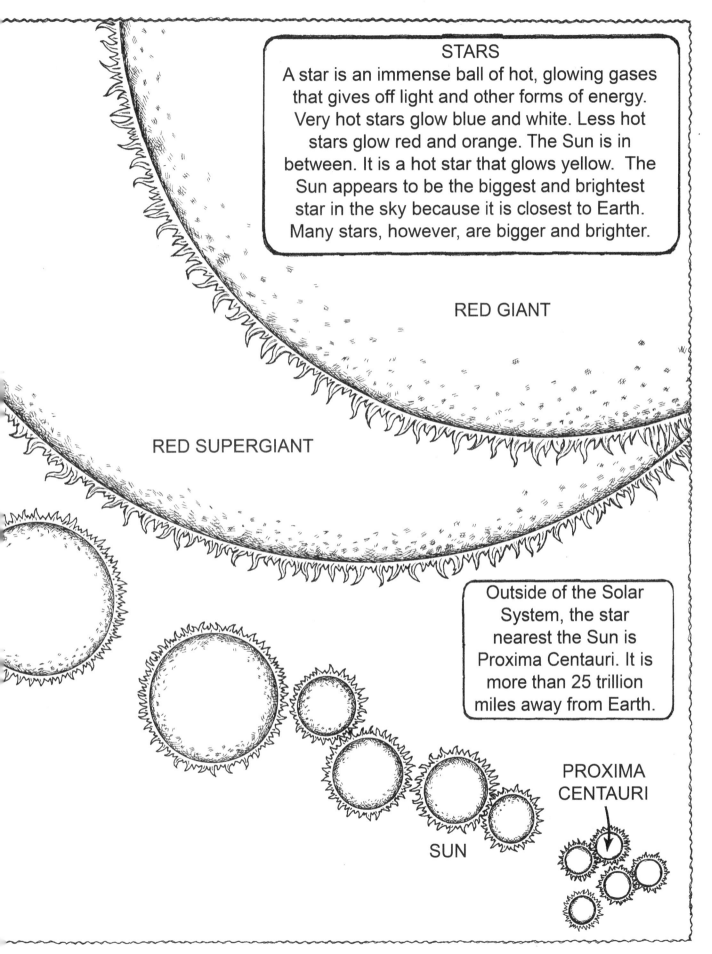

STARS

A star is an immense ball of hot, glowing gases that gives off light and other forms of energy. Very hot stars glow blue and white. Less hot stars glow red and orange. The Sun is in between. It is a hot star that glows yellow. The Sun appears to be the biggest and brightest star in the sky because it is closest to Earth. Many stars, however, are bigger and brighter.

RED GIANT

RED SUPERGIANT

Outside of the Solar System, the star nearest the Sun is Proxima Centauri. It is more than 25 trillion miles away from Earth.

SUN

PROXIMA CENTAURI

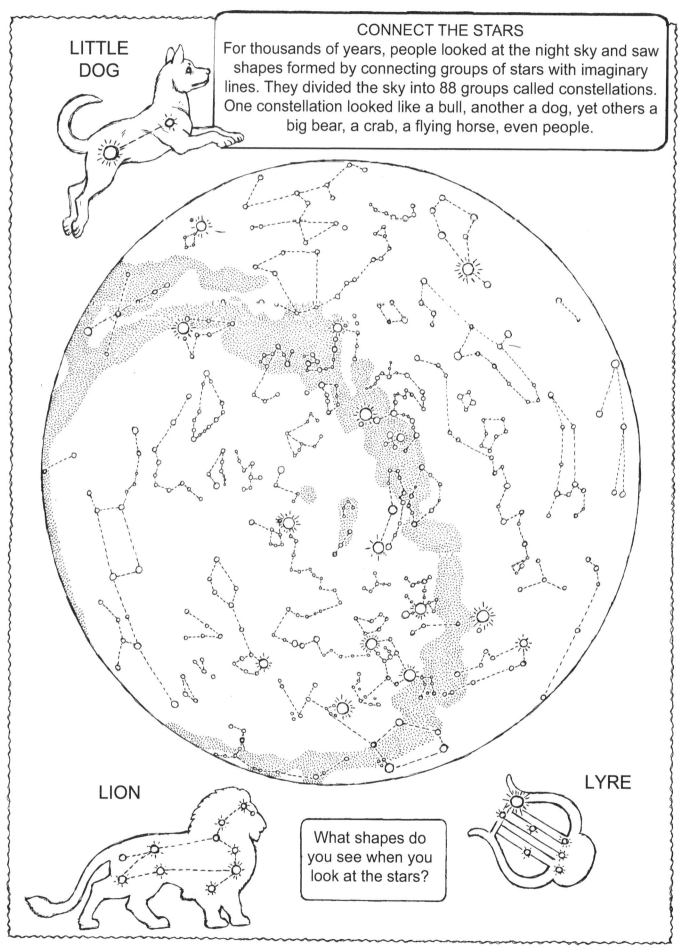

LITTLE DOG

CONNECT THE STARS
For thousands of years, people looked at the night sky and saw shapes formed by connecting groups of stars with imaginary lines. They divided the sky into 88 groups called constellations. One constellation looked like a bull, another a dog, yet others a big bear, a crab, a flying horse, even people.

LION

What shapes do you see when you look at the stars?

LYRE

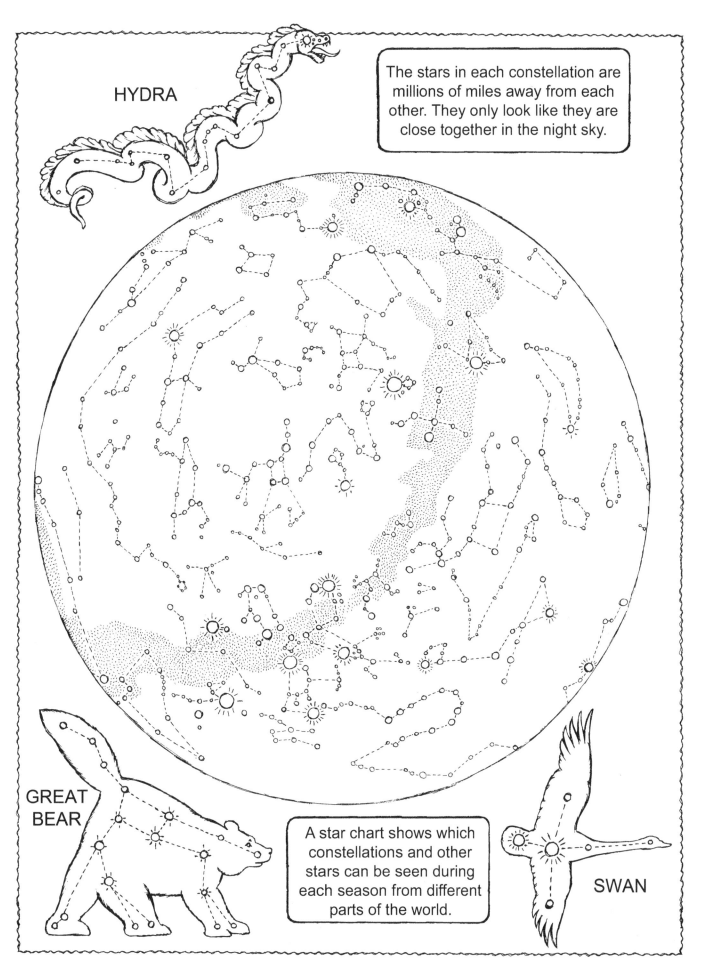

HYDRA

The stars in each constellation are millions of miles away from each other. They only look like they are close together in the night sky.

GREAT BEAR

A star chart shows which constellations and other stars can be seen during each season from different parts of the world.

SWAN

31

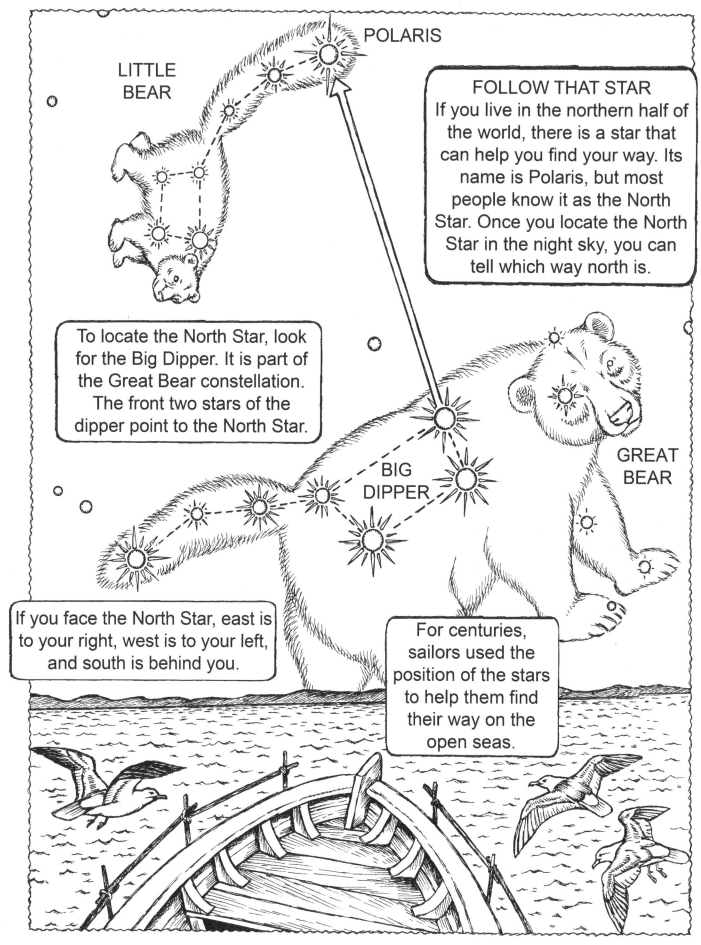

POLARIS

LITTLE BEAR

FOLLOW THAT STAR
If you live in the northern half of the world, there is a star that can help you find your way. Its name is Polaris, but most people know it as the North Star. Once you locate the North Star in the night sky, you can tell which way north is.

To locate the North Star, look for the Big Dipper. It is part of the Great Bear constellation. The front two stars of the dipper point to the North Star.

BIG DIPPER

GREAT BEAR

If you face the North Star, east is to your right, west is to your left, and south is behind you.

For centuries, sailors used the position of the stars to help them find their way on the open seas.

TELESCOPES
On a clear night you can see a lot of stars in the night sky. With a telescope, you can see thousands more. A telescope lets you see things your eyes alone can't. A telescope makes stars, planets, and moons seem closer than they really are.

In 2018, the James Webb Space Telescope will replace the Hubble.

In 1990 the Hubble Space Telescope was launched into orbit. The Hubble telescope has sent back to Earth hundreds of thousands of photographs of stars, planets, and other galaxies.

Portable telescopes and giant telescopes in observatories view the stars from Earth.

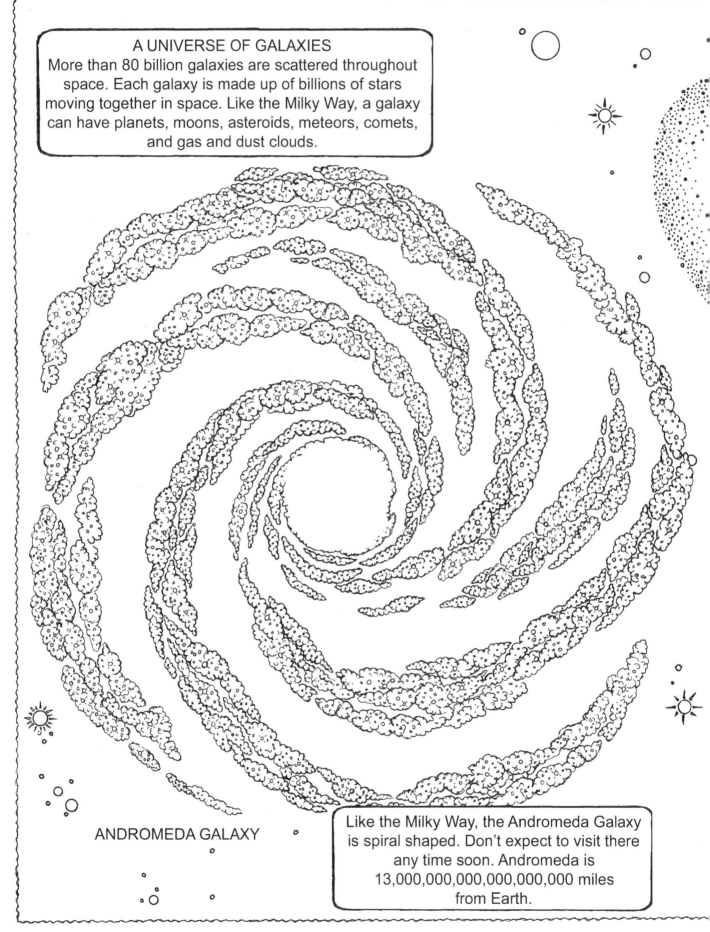

A UNIVERSE OF GALAXIES
More than 80 billion galaxies are scattered throughout space. Each galaxy is made up of billions of stars moving together in space. Like the Milky Way, a galaxy can have planets, moons, asteroids, meteors, comets, and gas and dust clouds.

ANDROMEDA GALAXY

Like the Milky Way, the Andromeda Galaxy is spiral shaped. Don't expect to visit there any time soon. Andromeda is 13,000,000,000,000,000,000 miles from Earth.

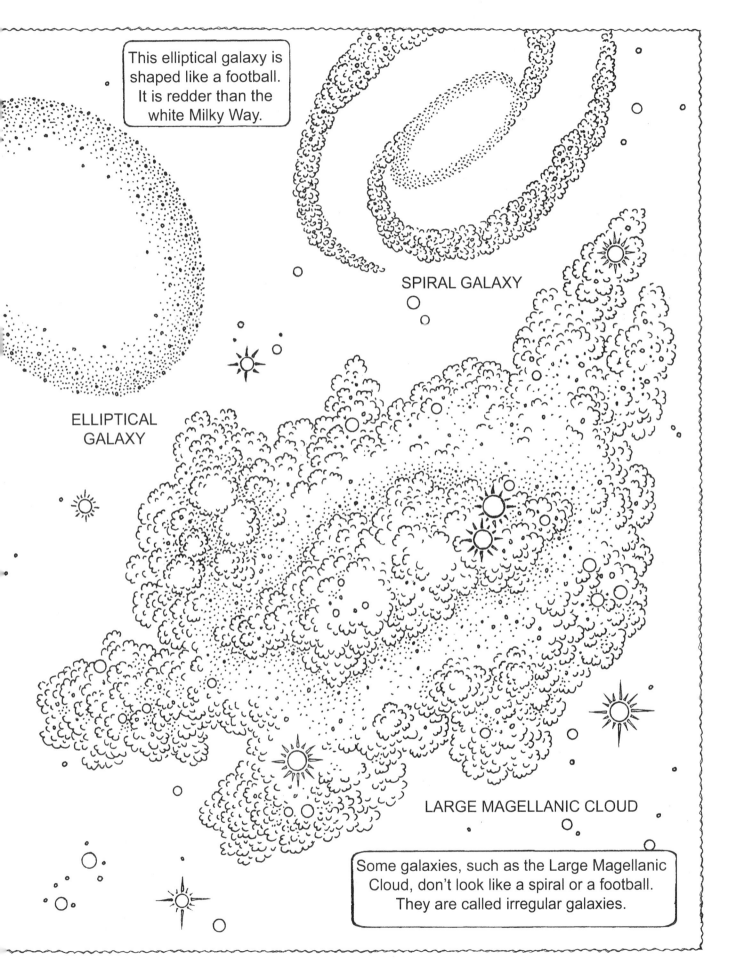

This elliptical galaxy is shaped like a football. It is redder than the white Milky Way.

SPIRAL GALAXY

ELLIPTICAL GALAXY

LARGE MAGELLANIC CLOUD

Some galaxies, such as the Large Magellanic Cloud, don't look like a spiral or a football. They are called irregular galaxies.

Stars born in the Great Orion Nebula shine brightly as blue giant and blue supergiant stars.

GREAT ORION NEBULA

Part of the Horsehead Nebula is in the shape of a horse's head.

BIRTH OF A STAR
When a star explodes, it leaves behind clouds of swirling dust and gases. Such clouds, called nebulas, may swirl for billions of years. But, if a shock wave from another exploding star hits, the dust and gases can clump together, spin faster, and superheat. When the temperature reaches a few million degrees, a star is born.

HORSEHEAD NEBULA

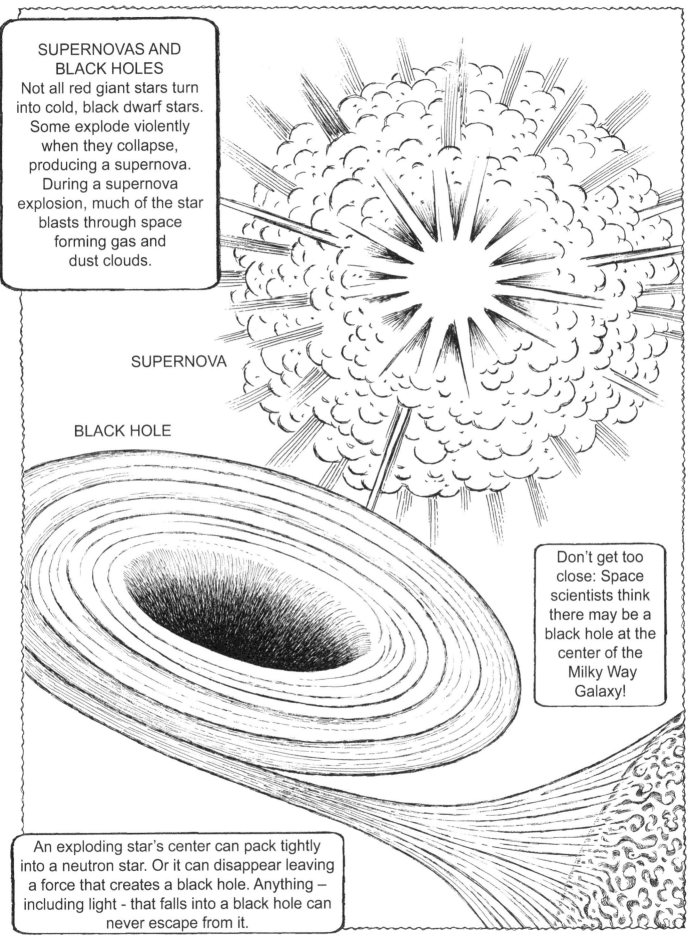

SUPERNOVAS AND BLACK HOLES

Not all red giant stars turn into cold, black dwarf stars. Some explode violently when they collapse, producing a supernova. During a supernova explosion, much of the star blasts through space forming gas and dust clouds.

SUPERNOVA

BLACK HOLE

Don't get too close: Space scientists think there may be a black hole at the center of the Milky Way Galaxy!

An exploding star's center can pack tightly into a neutron star. Or it can disappear leaving a force that creates a black hole. Anything – including light - that falls into a black hole can never escape from it.

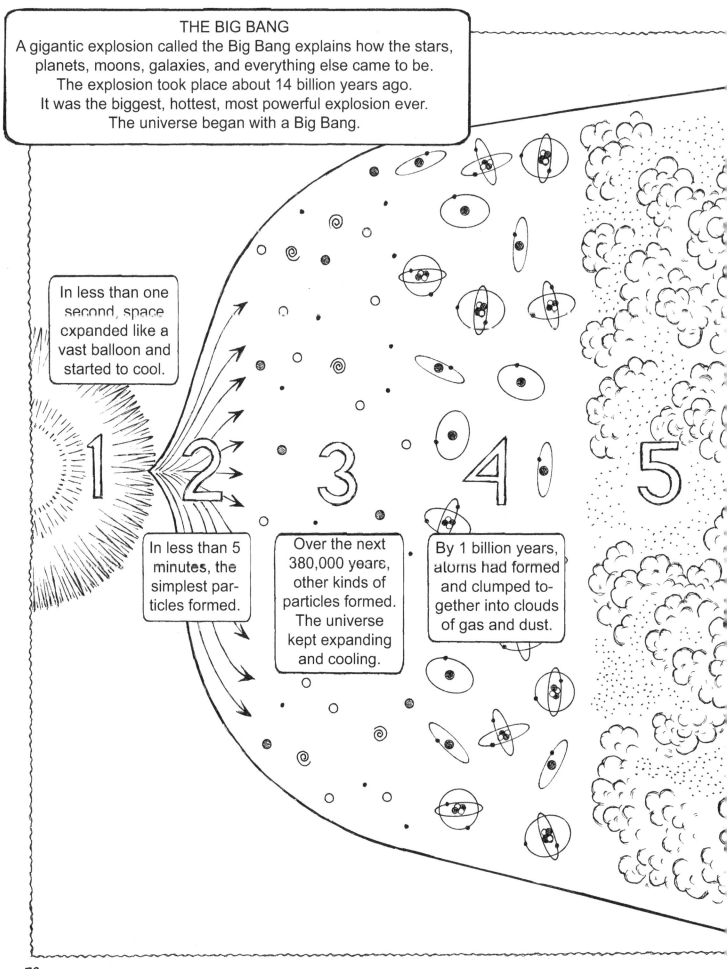

THE BIG BANG
A gigantic explosion called the Big Bang explains how the stars, planets, moons, galaxies, and everything else came to be. The explosion took place about 14 billion years ago. It was the biggest, hottest, most powerful explosion ever. The universe began with a Big Bang.

In less than one second, space expanded like a vast balloon and started to cool.

In less than 5 minutes, the simplest particles formed.

Over the next 380,000 years, other kinds of particles formed. The universe kept expanding and cooling.

By 1 billion years, atoms had formed and clumped together into clouds of gas and dust.

The gas and dust clouds collapsed under the force of gravity. Stars formed in the first galaxies and started to shine. The universe kept getting bigger and bigger.

Today, 13 billion years later, the universe is still increasing in size. It is made up of stars, planets, moons, space rocks, gases, and dust. It is also made up of mysterious dark energy and dark matter that no one has yet seen or understands. Maybe you will be the first person to figure out what dark matter and energy are and what they do.

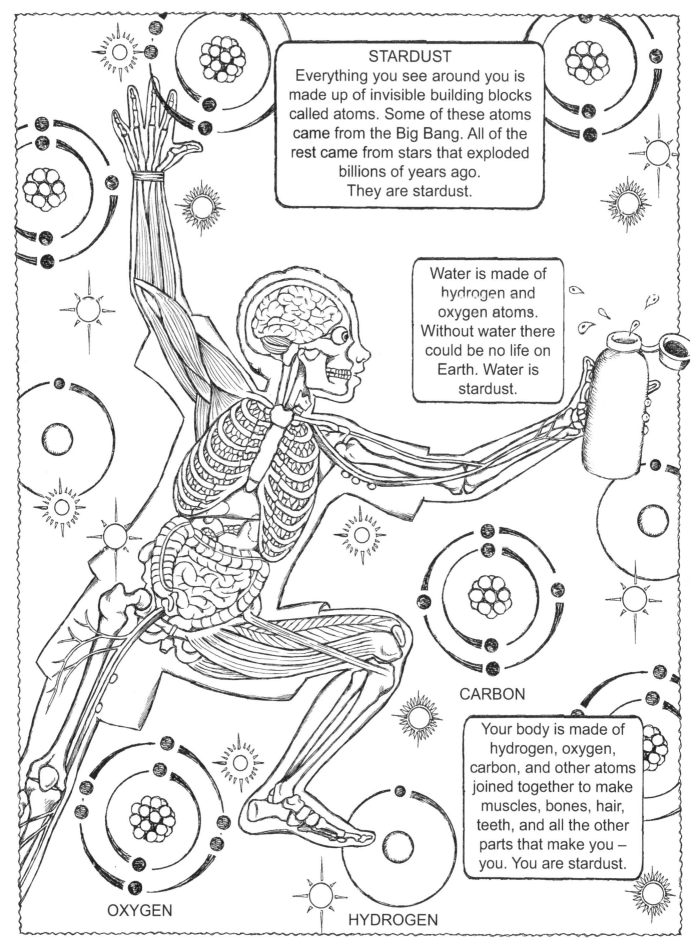

STARDUST
Everything you see around you is made up of invisible building blocks called atoms. Some of these atoms came from the Big Bang. All of the rest came from stars that exploded billions of years ago.
They are stardust.

Water is made of hydrogen and oxygen atoms. Without water there could be no life on Earth. Water is stardust.

CARBON

Your body is made of hydrogen, oxygen, carbon, and other atoms joined together to make muscles, bones, hair, teeth, and all the other parts that make you — you. You are stardust.

OXYGEN

HYDROGEN

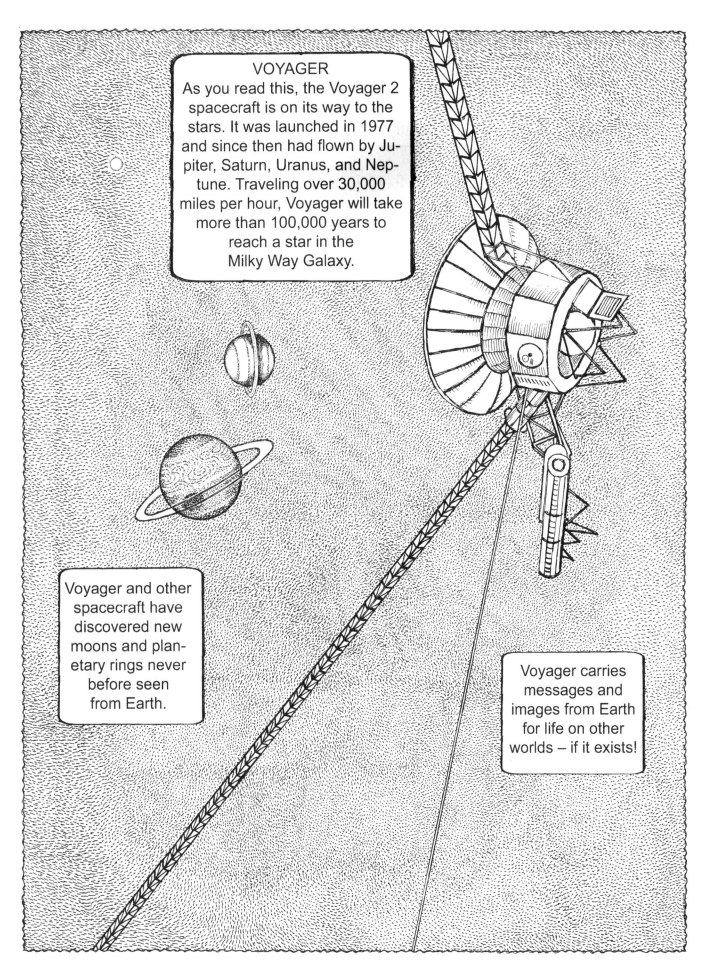

VOYAGER
As you read this, the Voyager 2 spacecraft is on its way to the stars. It was launched in 1977 and since then had flown by Jupiter, Saturn, Uranus, and Neptune. Traveling over 30,000 miles per hour, Voyager will take more than 100,000 years to reach a star in the Milky Way Galaxy.

Voyager and other spacecraft have discovered new moons and planetary rings never before seen from Earth.

Voyager carries messages and images from Earth for life on other worlds – if it exists!

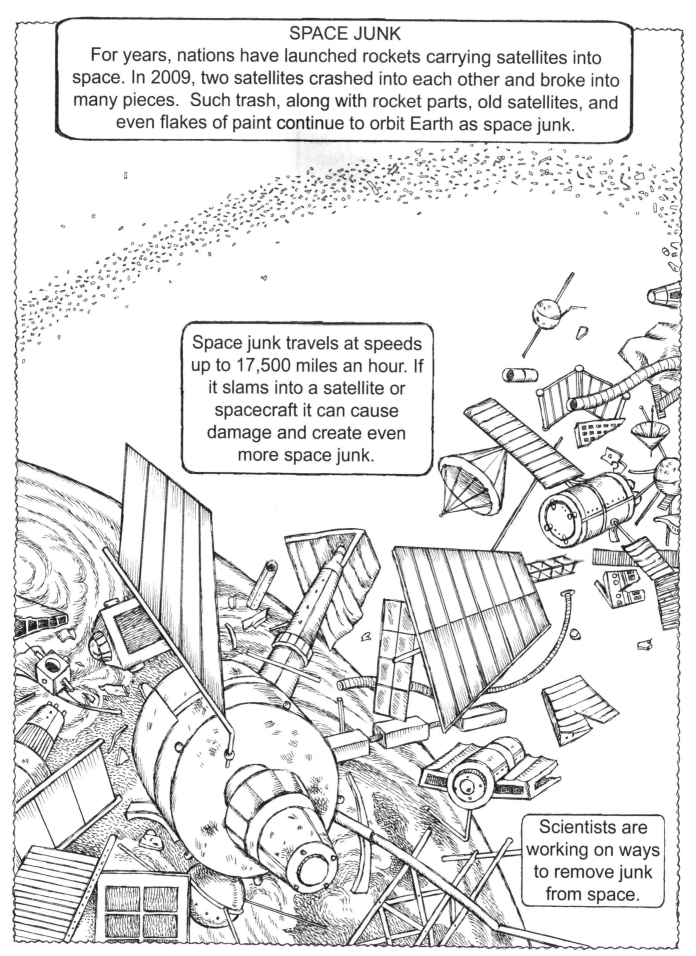

SPACE JUNK
For years, nations have launched rockets carrying satellites into space. In 2009, two satellites crashed into each other and broke into many pieces. Such trash, along with rocket parts, old satellites, and even flakes of paint continue to orbit Earth as space junk.

Space junk travels at speeds up to 17,500 miles an hour. If it slams into a satellite or spacecraft it can cause damage and create even more space junk.

Scientists are working on ways to remove junk from space.

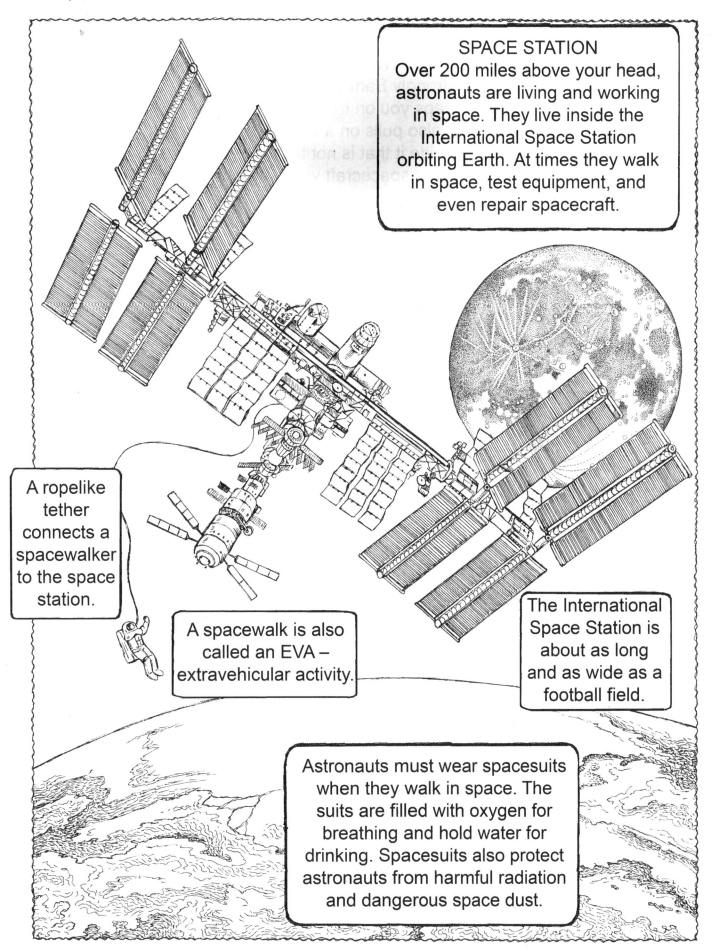

SPACE STATION
Over 200 miles above your head, astronauts are living and working in space. They live inside the International Space Station orbiting Earth. At times they walk in space, test equipment, and even repair spacecraft.

A ropelike tether connects a spacewalker to the space station.

A spacewalk is also called an EVA – extravehicular activity.

The International Space Station is about as long and as wide as a football field.

Astronauts must wear spacesuits when they walk in space. The suits are filled with oxygen for breathing and hold water for drinking. Spacesuits also protect astronauts from harmful radiation and dangerous space dust.

FLOATING IN SPACE

How much do you weigh? Whatever the number of pounds, your weight tells you how **strongly Earth's** gravity is pulling down on you. The force of gravity **keeps you** on the ground and not floating in the air. Earth's gravity **also pulls on a spacecraft** orbiting Earth. Anything inside it that **is not tied** down floats. If you were on a **spacecraft** you would float, too.

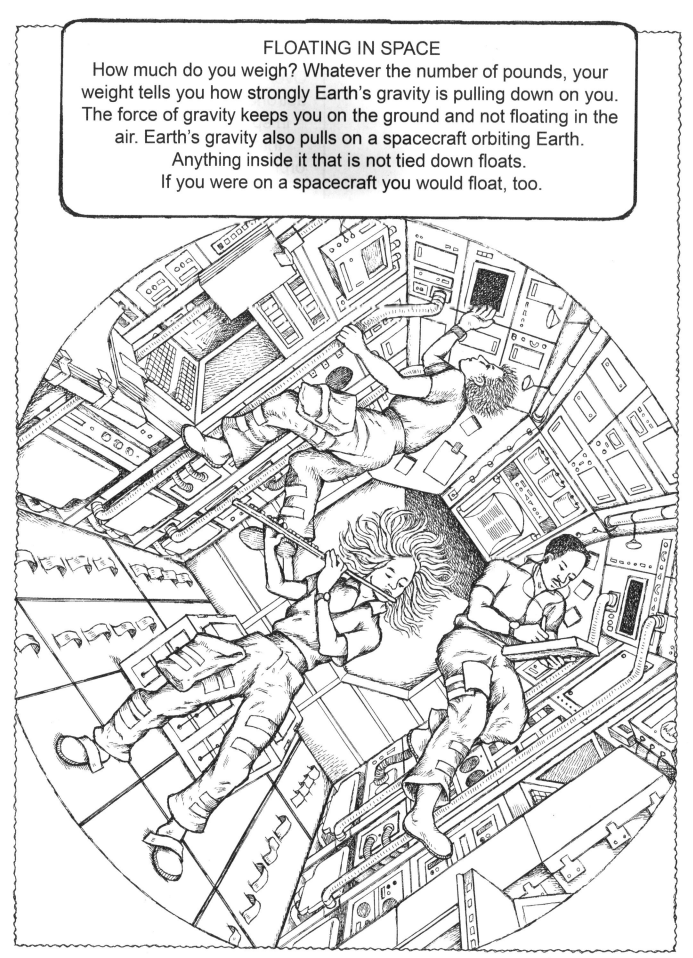

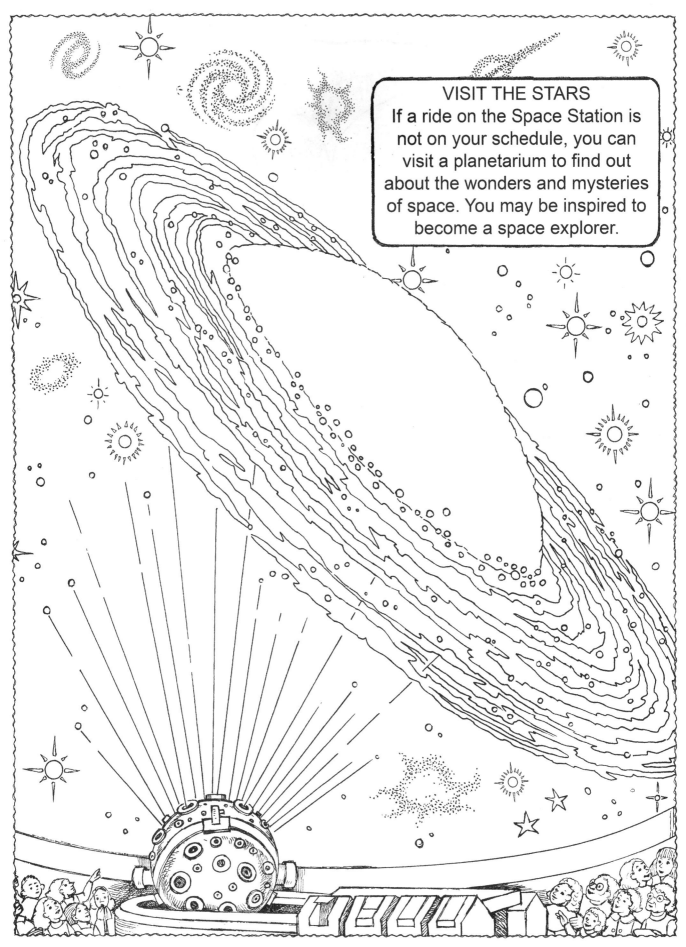

VISIT THE STARS
If a ride on the Space Station is not on your schedule, you can visit a planetarium to find out about the wonders and mysteries of space. You may be inspired to become a space explorer.

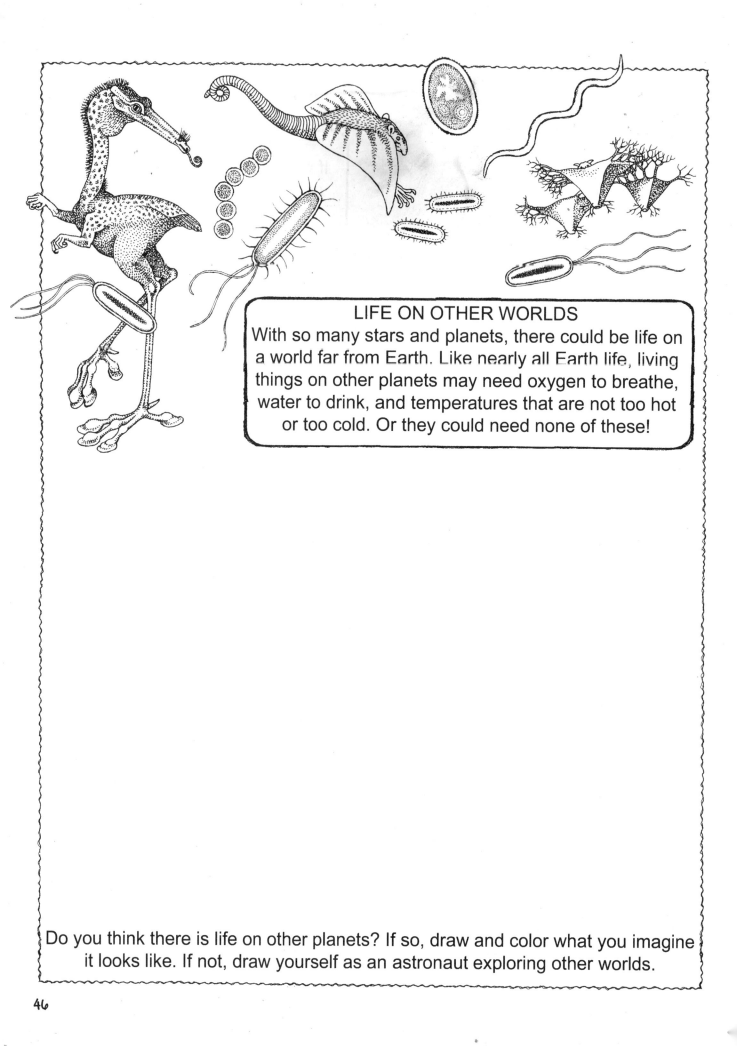

LIFE ON OTHER WORLDS
With so many stars and planets, there could be life on a world far from Earth. Like nearly all Earth life, living things on other planets may need oxygen to breathe, water to drink, and temperatures that are not too hot or too cold. Or they could need none of these!

Do you think there is life on other planets? If so, draw and color what you imagine it looks like. If not, draw yourself as an astronaut exploring other worlds.